Patterns

BY SARA PISTOIA

Published by The Child's World®
1980 Lookout Drive • Mankato, MN 56003-1705
800-599-READ • www.childsworld.com

Acknowledgments
The Child's World®: Mary Berendes, Publishing Director
The Design Lab: Design
Editing: Jody Jensen Shaffer

Photographs ©: Photodisc: cover, 1, 4, 8, 24;
all other photographs David M. Budd Photography.

ISBN 9781623235338
LCCN 2013931433

Printed in the United States of America
Mankato, MN
July, 2013
PA02173

ABOUT THE AUTHOR

Sara Pistoia is a retired elementary teacher living in Southern California with her husband and a variety of pets. In authoring this series, she draws on the experience of many years of teaching first and second graders.

Patterns

We use **patterns** to **recognize** all kinds of things in our world. Colors or shapes used over and over form a pattern.

You can see patterns on wrapping paper. You can see patterns on leaves and flowers.

These patterns are on animal fur. Can you guess which animals they are?

The world would be different without patterns.
Without stripes, this zebra would look like a horse!

Tigers and leopards are both wild cats. Is this a tiger or a leopard? You can tell by the stripes on its fur. Tigers have stripes. Leopards have spots.

Patterns can be made with shapes, sizes, colors, and **positions**.

Look at the animal on the next page. You know it's a panda because it looks like a panda. But what makes a panda look different from a grizzly bear?

A panda's black and white coloring forms a pattern. That pattern makes the panda look different from every other animal.

Pandas have white faces with black patches around their eyes. Where else do you see black patches?

Sometimes the parts of a pattern **repeat** themselves. When patterns repeat, it helps us think about what might come next.

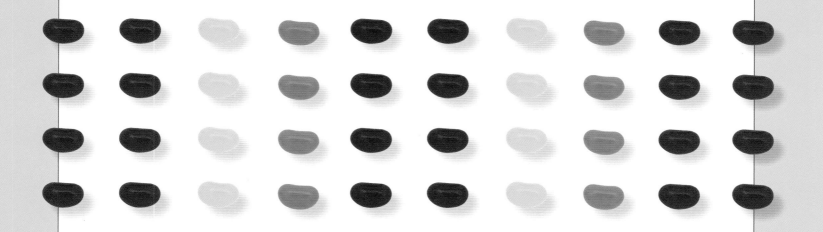

These jelly beans form a pattern. The pattern uses colors and numbers. How can you tell what color comes next?

To figure out which color jelly bean comes next, think about the order of the colors you see. Next, count how many of each color there are. Red, red, yellow, green. Red, red, yellow, green.

Some patterns are simple, like the stripes on this snake. Do you see the pattern? Red, black, yellow, black. Red, black, yellow, black.

Some patterns aren't so simple. This wrapping paper has a pattern, but it keeps changing. Can you tell what might come next?

It's hard to know what would come next in this pattern!

Knowing about patterns can help us in math class. You already know some patterns in math. When you count, you use a pattern:

0, 1, 2, 3, 4, 5, 6, 7, 8, 9...

What comes next?

Did you say "10"? You're right!

What happens when we reach 10? The pattern starts all over again!

But this time, we put a "**1**" in front of each number—10, 11….

Do you see the pattern?

10, 11, 12, 13, 14, 15, 16, 17, 18, 19...

Now try **counting** the peanuts on the next page. What happens when we reach 19? We start the pattern all over again at 20.

Can you think of the last four numbers in the pattern?

What comes after 6? What comes after 16? Now think about what comes after 26.

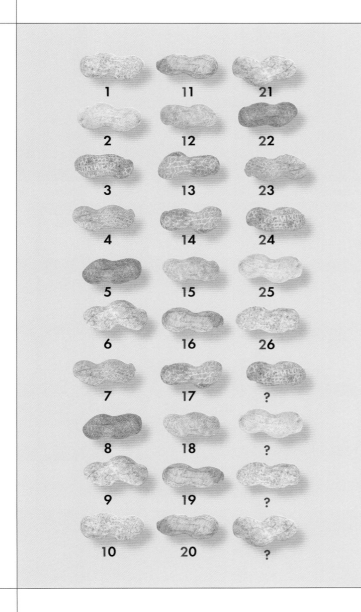

The last four numbers are 27, 28, 29, and 30. Did the pattern change after 29? Yes!

We used the number 3 and started the pattern all over again!

The days of the week form a pattern, too.

Which day always comes after Sunday?

Which day always comes after Wednesday?

Monday	Tuesday	Wednesday	Thursday	Friday	Saturday	Sunday
		1	2	3	4	5
6	7	8	9	10	11	12
13	14	15	16	17	18	19
20	21	22	23	24	25	26
27	28	29	30			

September

Knowing the days of the week can help you **solve** this math problem:

Let's say you leave home on Saturday to go to your grandma's house. It will take four days to get there. On what day will you arrive?

Saturday, Sunday, Monday, Tuesday—you'll be there Tuesday.

Look at the **hundreds** chart on the next page. Do you see patterns that can help you with math?

Count the numbers with yellow jelly beans. You are counting by **fives**. What about the last row? Do you know where to place the jelly beans to finish the pattern?

1	2	3	4	5	6	7	8	9	10
11	12	13	14	15	16	17	18	19	20
21	22	23	24	25	26	27	28	29	30
31	32	33	34	35	36	37	38	39	40
41	42	43	44	45	46	47	48	49	50
51	52	53	54	55	56	57	58	59	60
61	62	63	64	65	66	67	68	69	70
71	72	73	74	75	76	77	78	79	80
81	82	83	84	85	86	87	88	89	90
91	92	93	94	95	96	97	98	99	100

The yellow jelly bean numbers on this chart make a pattern that counts by fives. Study the pattern. The numbers in the last row must be 95 and 100!

This musician thinks about patterns when he plays or writes music. Scientists think about finding patterns when they study plants. Artists think about patterns when they create a work of art.

Patterns of letters helped you learn to read. Discovering and using patterns is important in math, too.

If you start thinking about patterns, you can see them everywhere!

Key Words

counting
fives
hundreds
patterns
positions
recognize
repeat
solve

Index